UP, DOWN, SIDEWAYS

THE IMPACT OF NOVEMBER 2018'S MID-TERM ELECTION ON THE STOCK MARKET AND DOW INDEX

DALE ALLMAN

1. What is the Dow Jones Index?

The Dow Jones Industrial Average (DJIA), is the leading 30 Blue Chip stocks whose performance is balanced daily of trading on the securities market. The components of the Dow Jones reads like a who's who in the stock exchange.

Presently, the leading 30 supplies are doing fairly well on the stock market. Due to the handful of stocks that make up the DJIA all it takes it a few of the stocks to take waver or falter and then the overall average can struggle or move sideways. Let's take a look at the individual companies that make up the DJIA.

Here is the list of most recent 30 industrials included in the index, according to CNN Money:

MMM 3M	INTC Intel
AXP American Express	JNJ Johnson & Johnson
AAPL Apple	JPM JPMorgan Chase
BA Boeing	MCD McDonald's
CAT Caterpillar	MRK Merck
CVX Chevron	MSFT Microsoft
CSCO Cisco	NKE Nike
KO Coca-Cola	PFE Pfizer
DIS Disney	PG Procter & Gamble
DWDP DowDuPont Inc	TRV Travelers Companies Inc
XOM Exxon Mobil	UTX United Technologies
GS Goldman Sachs	UNH UnitedHealth
HD Home Depot	VZ Verizon
IBM IBM	V Visa
	WMT Wal-Mart
	WBA Walgreen

It ought to be no shock to a lot of people that Wal-Mart Inc is a component of the Dow Jones Industrial. Another strong past performer Home Depot also included, as is McDonald's. Disney represents several verticals including film, resorts, and entertainment services and so on. It also has a significant worldwide footprint.

Modern technology and high-tech innovation is represented by Microsoft, United Technologies, Hewlett-Packard, Verizon, International Business Machines, and Intel.

The index strives to represent multiple facets of the US economy and the scope of its international companies, based in America. Basic materials, medicines, machinery, cars, and financial services are all represented. As are airlines, heavy equipment, oil & gas, retail, credit cards and retail pharmacies.

The construction of the actual index is often described as a weighted average of prices for one share of stock from all 30 companies included in the index. Basically what that means is that the share prices (in real time that can mean this moment, throughout the day, at the end of the day, this week, and so on) are added together. Then that total or sum is divided by a "divisor" to create the index.

The "divisor" while derivable from the numbers available today, is usually not a matter of concern when we look at daily, weekly or monthly movements in the Dow Index. Typically over a short-term period (e.g. several months) the "divisor" will remain the same or stay constant. Adjustments usually take place based on stock splits or other adjustments made by individual companies.

So, what's important to track as we look at and evaluate the stock market is the overall level of the Dow Index, changes over time, and any related trends (up or down or sideways).

Certainly we can look at and evaluate each individual stock price that makes up the overall index. And, we can watch and track the index overall.

(Ticker Symbol) Company	Share Price	(Ticker Symbol) Company	Share Price
MMM 3M	$ 190.26	JNJ Johnson & Johnson	$ 139.99
AXP American Express	$ 102.73	JPM JPMorgan Chase	$ 109.02
AAPL Apple	$ 218.86	MCD McDonald's	$ 176.90
BA Boeing	$ 354.86	MRK Merck	$ 73.61
CAT Caterpillar	$ 121.32	MSFT Microsoft	$ 106.81
CVX Chevron	$ 111.65	NKE Nike	$ 75.04
CSCO Cisco	$ 45.75	PFE Pfizer	$ 43.06
KO Coca-Cola	$ 47.88	PG Procter & Gamble	$ 88.68
DIS Disney	$ 114.83	TRV Travelers Companies Inc	$ 125.13
DWDP DowDuPont Inc	$ 53.92	UTX United Technologies	$ 124.21
XOM Exxon Mobil	$ 79.68	UNH UnitedHealth	$ 261.35
GS Goldman Sachs	$ 225.37	VZ Verizon	$ 57.09
HD Home Depot	$ 175.88	V Visa	$ 137.85
IBM IBM	$ 115.43	WMT Wal-Mart	$ 100.28
INTC Intel	$ 46.88	WBA Walgreen	$ 79.77

The above table shows the most recent share prices (USD per one share) for each of the 30 companies included in the Dow Index. The lowest price is Pfizer at $43.06 per share and the highest price is Boeing at $354.86 per share. These prices are quoted as of 4:15 pm EST on October 31, 2018, after the market close but before any after-hours trading.

When the Dow Index first started in the 1800s the index was calculated as a simple arithmetic average – add up all 30 share prices and divide that total by 30. As the Index gained in popularity, it became clear that the simple average gave too much emphasis to the larger prices. To correct for this potential bias, a weighted approach was added.

In addition to the Dow Index, there are several other summary indices or measures of overall stock market activity. Better known index values that are tracked regularly include the S&P 500 (Standard & Poor's index of 500 stocks) and the NASDAQ (National Association of Securities Dealers Automated Quotations). While the Dow is the most popular, it has different uses and tends to represent a narrower view of the equities markets. With 500 stocks, the S&P naturally has a broader view. And the NASDAQ index represents smaller or younger companies. The NASDAQ tracks about 4,000 individual stocks and their share prices as part of that index.

For individual investors, you cannot trade the actual index values of the Dow, S&P or NASDAQ. In the past, if you wanted your investments to track with the market, about the only way you could do that would be to buy shares of each of the 30 stocks (in the Dow for example) or select a "representative" group of stocks for the S&P or NASDAQ indices. Recently, though, what are called index funds have been created. These ETFs as they are called (Exchange Traded Funds) were first traded in Canada in 1990 and then started trading in the United States in 1993.

The reason we track the Dow or similar index values is to guage the overall health of the country's stocks and the underlying companies that issue them. One way to get a "read" on how we are doing, is to look at the Dow Index over time. We'll take that up next and examine some of the recent trends and changes in the Dow for the past several years.

2. Tracking the Stock Exchange

A bear market is a decreasing market. It has a tendency to start with a sharp decline in supply rates throughout the board. There is typically an eye in the tornado, throughout which supply rates boost.

A bull market is a climbing market. In a bull market, capitalists are favorable. When companies earnings, financiers require to share an item of the pie-- they acquire supplies as well as hang on limited to view the cash roll in.

You have actually seen motion pictures in which frenzied supply investors are purchasing a thousand shares of a warm supply or unloading shares of a plunging supply. You have actually seen commercials for broker agent companies that assert to have interesting leads as well as solid profiles. As well as you have actually possibly listened to a hundred various methods to anticipate the fluctuations of the stock exchange.

Exactly how do these investors as well as companies anticipate which shares will strike large? Exactly how do they recognize when to market?

The reality exists is no enchanting method to forecast the securities market. Several concerns impact fluctuates in share rates, whether steady modifications or sharp spikes. The most effective method to comprehend exactly how the marketplace changes is to examine fads.

In this write-up we will certainly review securities market fads, which aid capitalists determine what supplies to purchase and also when. Keeping an eye on growths as well as drop-offs over the background of specific supplies, in addition to recognizing market-wide patterns, aids financiers intend dealing.

Numerous elements influence rates in the stock exchange, consisting of rising cost of living, rate of interest, power costs, oil costs and also worldwide concerns, such as battle, criminal offense, scams and also political agitation.

Supply market patterns are like the actions of an individual. Acknowledging a pattern in the supply market or in a private supply will certainly allow you to pick the finest times to purchase as well as market.

Simply what makes those ticker numbers transform?

Numerous capitalists market their supply since they think the supply is worth much less as well as is just going to lower in rate. As the need for the supply lowers, the rate of the supply reduces. When this takes place to lots of business in the supply market, the supply market experiences a descending change.

When customers do not get points as well as companies do not expand, business' earnings reduce, creating a supply cost decline. Alternatively, when the Federal Get reduces the passion price, financiers have a tendency to obtain thrilled. Capitalists often tend to purchase, acquire, purchase!

Perhaps after a while, individuals expand worn out of widgets as well as desire to acquire the brand-new whatsit rather. As you saw with rising cost of living and also passion prices, when a business reports reduced earnings, capitalists shed self-confidence in the business and also offer their supply, which reduces the worth of the supply.

- Power Rates: Individuals constantly require power. Just significant modifications in power expenses have a considerable impact on the supply market.

Others maintain paying the high rate yet, as an outcome, get less customer products. The supply market has a tendency to respond adversely to high oil costs.

- International and also Domestic Issues: Battle has a tendency to influence the supply market adversely. Companies make much less cash. Financiers have a tendency to unload their supplies, triggering a loss in the market.

- Anxiety: Besides hesitating of the marketplace effects of battle, oil costs or a government rate of interest trek, capitalists hesitate of shedding their loan. Capitalists often tend to do not like seeing their loan decrease as the cost of their shares lowers.

Nobody actually understands the specific beginning of the terms "bull" and also "bear" to explain the stock exchange, however their significance is clear. One of the most vital point to understand about these terms is that they define lasting fads, not temporary modifications. Bull and also bearishness are typically gauged in years.

In a bear market, the economic climate has a tendency to be weak. As we have actually seen, this cheapens an offered firm's supply. Financiers often tend to market their supplies prior to the worth lowers as well much.

Financial investment Approaches-- Exactly How to Trip the Bull and also Tame the Bear

The most effective technique to generate income in an advancing market is to identify the pattern early as well as make wise buys. Acquire reduced-- market high.

It might appear counterproductive that you can generate income throughout a bearish market. Below are a couple of means you can tame the bear:

Brief sell: A brief sell is a profession that includes obtaining supply you do not have, marketing it, waiting on the rate to drop, after that getting it back at a reduced rate, therefore acquiring revenue.

Purchase UNITED STATES Treasury bonds: Bond rates of interest have a tendency to climb throughout bearish market, that makes for an appealing possibility throughout a time of unpredictability

Get protective supplies: This is a low-risk means for capitalists to maintain their cash in the stock exchange. A protective supply is so called due to the fact that its worth does not change a lot. Energy supplies (power, water, and so on) are prominent protective supplies.

The Future

Background has actually revealed that the stock exchange constantly climbs over the long-term. Bearishness and also accidents occur, yet the marketplace constantly recovers as well as ultimately climbs more than it ever before was in the past.

Lots of expert capitalists state that establishing your financial investments entirely on the basis of whether the marketplace is favorable or bearish is foolish. It is much better to base financial investments on research study right into solid, qualified companies with lots of development capacity. Gradually, enlightened as well as notified financial investments have a tendency to make money greater than financial investments based upon report, worry, uncertainty and also superstitious notion.

You have actually seen films in which frenzied supply investors are purchasing a thousand shares of a warm supply or disposing shares of a plunging supply. Identifying a pattern in the supply market or in a specific supply will certainly allow you to select the finest times to get and also offer.

Lots of financiers offer their supply since they think the supply is worth much less and also is just going to reduce in rate. When this takes place to lots of business in the supply market, the supply market experiences a down change. Acquire protective supplies: This is a low-risk means for capitalists to maintain their loan in the supply market.

3. Recent DOW Trends

"One thing you can say with absolute certainty, in the future the stock market will move up, down or sideways."

The chart below shows the behavior and patterns of the Dow Jones Industrial Index (simply referred to as the Dow) from the beginning of 2016 through the end of October 2018.

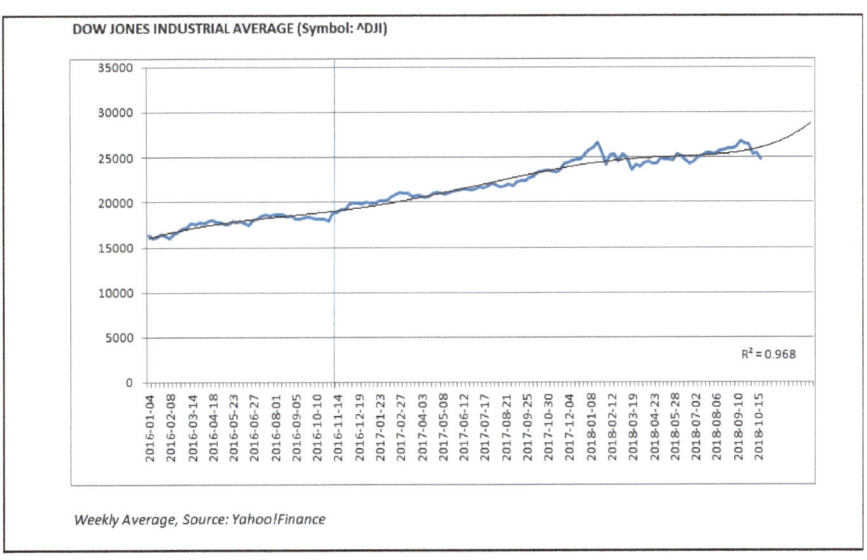

At the beginning of 2016, before that year's Presidential Election, the index started the year at a value of 16,346 (week of Jan 4 2016). By the time of the election (the vertical blue line on the chart), the overall index had risen to 18,847, an increase during the year of 15% from January through November 7th. There were some ups and downs during the year but overall the index increased.

After the election of President Donald J. Trump, the index grew to its most recent record high of 26,617 on the week of January 22, 2018, an increase of 41% since the election in November 2016. During that roughly 14 month period, there were different growth periods, and some month-to-month ups and downs, but generally the stock market increased during that period.

Since January of 2018 the index has tended to move more or less sideways. The second "peak" you can see on the chart was in the week of September 17, 2018 at an index value of 26,744, roughly the same as the top at January 22nd. And, since then the Dow Index has fallen to the most recent value of 24, 688 in the week of October 22, 2018, a 7.7% decline in the month between mid-September and mid-October.

These latest changes occurred in the stock market for several reasons. Recent interest rate increases by the Federal Reserve have been blamed by some. Rapid growth in the U.S. Economy during 2017 and most of 2018 is thought to have slowed. There may be some "profit taking" after the significant increase in stock prices over the past two years. Many people may be selling stocks and putting the cash from their sales into other accounts – preparing for holiday shopping, for example. And, historically over several years, the month of October has not been a good month for seeing increases in the Dow index or stock prices.

The chart we included above also has a "trend" line included to show you the pattern of behavior since the beginning of 2016 (the black wavy line on the chart). This trend line reflects one of the best ways to begin to look at what's most likely to happen to the market (or the Dow Index) in the near future. Predicting the Dow is the subject of our next chapter.

4. Concept of stock exchange forecasting

Projecting the stock market is every financier's dream. The acquainted proverb, "Acquire low, sell high," is basic sufficient, but timing the lows and the highs is an obstacle. Determining the patterns in the marketplace is the basis for all forecasting methods. Financiers ton of money fluctuate with their capability to time their transactions appropriately.

Technical Analysis

The majority of projecting systems are constructed around technological evaluation, which postulates that patterns in the stock market repeat themselves. If an investor can interpret the pattern correctly, then he can forecast what the future instructions will be. Most patterns in a bull market are additionally in a bearish market just inverted. Investors attempt to determine a support level below which a stock cost is not likely to drop-- and also if it does, it might fall far more. A resistance level is a greater price that is difficult to pass through. Chart fans identify head-and-shoulder formations, up patterns, down trends, tops, bases and also even more. Another method that investors follow are moving standards. By plotting relocating standards of different periods-- 20-day, 50-day as well as 200-day, as an example-- financiers can identify deal points.

Dow Theory

According to Dow Theory there are three fads in market movements. In the case of a bull market in each trend both averages should close greater than the previous high. In the instance of a bear market both standards need to close reduced than the previous reduced to establish a bear market.

Elliott Wave Theory

Established by Ralph Elliott in the 1920s, this concept additionally recommends that the market relocates a collection of predictable waves. Each fad on the market includes five waves. In a bull market there are 3 impulse waves, each separated by a correction, none of which hideaway to the previous low. In a bearish market the trend is turned around, but following the exact same pattern. Within each wave there might be smaller sized sub-waves that fluctuate around the bigger trend. Because there are many waves as well as sub-waves involved, discovering the core trend lines is challenging.

Candlestick Charting

Candlestick charting is an alternative method to forecast stock movements. Task is typically outlined by day or week as a figure looking like a candlestick. Completions of the "wick" inform the high and low rate for the period. Completions of the "candle" inform where the supply opened as well as closed. The candle is solid if the stock folded as well as open up if it closed through. Forecasters that use this technique look for patterns and patterns. A brief examination of a candle holder chart can likewise expose patterns in price volatility. Candle holder charting can be enhanced with various other technical evaluation tools such as moving averages.

The majority of patterns in a bull market are additionally in a bear market only inverted. According to Dow Theory there are 3 patterns in market activities. In the case of a bull market in each pattern both standards have to close higher than the previous high. In the instance of a bear market both standards have to close reduced than the previous low to develop a bear market.

5. Determining Patterns In The Securities Market

1. Forecast of the future

Actual Pyschics would certainly, without a doubt, help people investing in stocks. Much of investors and also brokers time is invested attempting to predict what the marketplace will certainly do in the following couple of days to months. Nevertheless, the process is not all speculative presuming. If one pays close attention, the marketplace will really indicate which way it is going. Finding out about forecasting the market can considerably profit anyone.

2. Instructions of market

You can see how a stock may do by studying the market. If the stock market is experiencing a period of development (a bull market) most stocks will gradually expand. If the stock market is in a decline (a bear market) most stocks will slowly lose value.

3. Establishing prices

To determine price, capitalists and brokers use the large three indicators: the Dow Jones Index, the S & P 500 and also the NASDAQ. These indications help capitalists and also brokers identify whether the market is going to continue in the existing fad or turn around program.

4. Finding volume

The day-to-day sales quantity of the markets is often utilized to understand quantity. If the market has experienced a high-volume day when values are up (on the 3 indexes), usually after that the market is up.

You can see how an individual stock could do by researching the market. Many, if not all, stocks move with the market. If the supply market is experience a period of development (a bull market) most stocks will gradually grow. If the stock market is in a decline (a bear market) most stockes will gradually lose worth. If the market has actually experienced a high-volume day and also prices are up (on the 3 indexes) after that the market is up.

6. Technical Analysis-- A Guide To Effective Trading

Worry not as you work with yet one more endeavor of your own. Participating in the trading market can both be complicated as well as easy. The pros and beginners alike require to constantly learn more about the pertinent steps to steer points in a really uncertain market. Yes, the trading globe is a really unpredictable one. You much better expect the most unforeseen things to take place. Without your recognizing, the presumption that you have made hrs ago already turns obsolete at this extremely minute. Therefore, an eager monitoring and watchful eyes are what you absolutely require to possess. On the other hand, your sensitivity to the modifications in the fad and also various other aspects controling the marketplace itself have to also be used.

An Excellent Check Out the Technical Indicators and also their Use

The very name emphasizes that technological indications are the mathematical solutions that indicate the existing as well as feasible patterns which influence the turn of events specifically those that have something to do with the stock costs. Technical analysts ideally make use of these signs to anticipate and conclude cycles which signal the moment period as to when it is best to either buy or offer an option, a supply, a security, or a product.

The indications are additionally determined depending upon the rate pattern of an acquired or supply. The gathered information consist of the quantity, highs, lows, shutting rate, as well as opening up cost. The cost data is frequently originated from the recent last periods of the stock's costs.

2 Main Types of Technical Indicators

Both main types are the lagging indicators and also the leading indicators. Keep reading to be familiar with their specific nature.

The delayed indicators are those that pursue the cost pattern of the stock, safety and security, or commodity. The information is then created from a past collection of data and are as a result reliable in denoting if a new pattern is presently establishing or whether the products are within the most effective trading arrays. The lagging indicators fall short in imagining pullbacks or rallies in the future.

The leading signs are able to forecast what may happen in the future. Accidents, pullbacks, or price rallies are easily identified given that they determine the movement of the cost's momentum. These tools are likewise able to specify rates that have gone expensive or also reduced thereby leading way to the terms overbought and also oversold.

In any case, both of these types are similarly significant. As a trader, it is a must that you are familiar with the patterns that establish in addition to the rate rallies, pullbacks, or stagnations. It is strongly recommended that as a capitalist, you have to get in touch with numerous technological indicators prior to making do with your conclusion or choice.

Other Tips for You

Below are a few various other tips that can lead you towards success in trading. Keep them in mind and incorporate them in your strategy.

Choose the technological indications with which you are most comfortable with. There are thousands of indications out there.

Back examine your recommended indicators using historical information. Think of a trading system that can aid you out in obtaining better outcomes for your picked indications.

Keep a close watch. Never ever idle. Always observe the performance of your supplies, safeties, or products.

Determine a particular stop loss. You should earn as opposed to lose cash. Choose the winning trading styles as well as methods and never amuse false hopes.

Last Words

Be smart. Be in harmony with the technical signs and the patterns that they show you. These are the simple suggestions that will put you on the ideal track.

The indicators are furthermore evaluated depending on the cost pattern of a derivative or stock. The delayed signs are those that go after the price pattern of the supply, safety, or product. It is strongly encouraged that as an investor, you have to get in touch with a number of technical indicators prior to making do with your verdict or choice.

Select the technical indicators with which you are most comfy with. Be in harmony with the technological indications and also the patterns that they show you.

7. Trend Analysis of Recent Dow Index

With this background, let's take another look at our most recent Dow Index chart and see if the trends or technical factors help us understand what direction the market is headed.

If you recall the trend we estimated looked like the market was headed up until recently. Reviewing the black trend line on the chart below, the circled part of our trend line suggests that from a recent value around 25,400 (where the black line intersects the blue line) up to a top value of near 29,000 at the end of the trend.

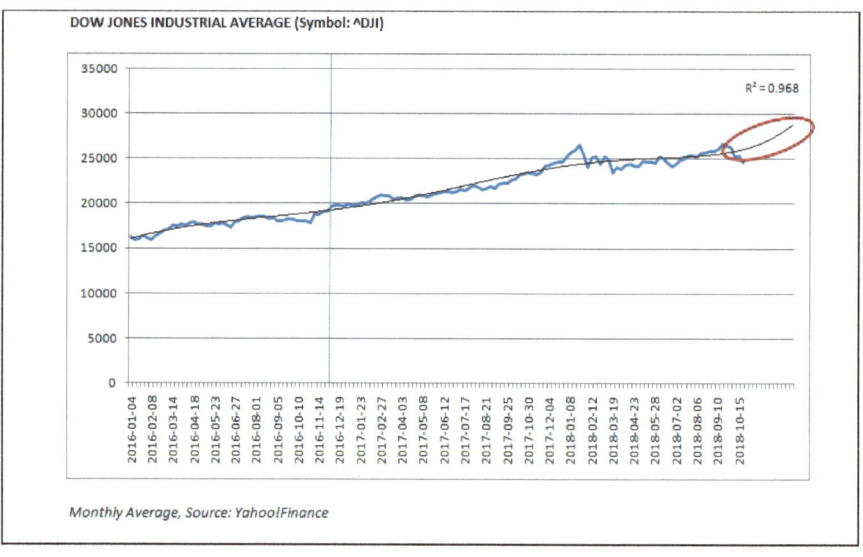

The top value would occur about 12 weeks after the last actual value in mid-October. That actual value (weekly average) was 25,400. Our trend suggests that the Dow Index will increase about 16% after the mid-November elections.

In fact, relative to historical stock market performance after mid-term elections, this trend result is only slightly more optimistic. Over the last 4 mid-terms (2014, 2010, 2006 and 2002), on average the Dow Index has increased 12-15%, only slightly below our trend.

The trend we estimated (polynomial, 6-degree adjustment) follows the patterns in the index and "fits" the data reasonable well. Note the R^2 (often called the R-squared) value of the equation. At 0.968 that means or can be interpreted to mean that we've explained almost 97% of the variation in the data. That is an extremely good result and lends some level of confidence in our trend forecast.

There does appear to be an exception, though, to the trend. During the period from January 22 to September 19, the market moved sideways (basically… some ups and downs, but a very narrow trading range). Since mid-September the index value has declined to just under 25,000 similar to the declines seen within the January to September period.

So the question is – and especially relative to the November 2018 mid-term elections – is the trend a true and accurate representation of the Dow such that we can rely on the forecasts provided by the trend equation estimates. There are several other tools and techniques we can use to evaluate the current and recent behavior of the Dow, analyze the patterns we see, and make additional forecasts or predictions of where we expect the stock market to be by the end of the year. These additional tools are the subjects of the next few chapters.

8.   Technical Analysis – Recent Trends

According to Investopedia, technical analysis is a trading discipline employed to evaluate investments and identify trading opportunities by analyzing statistical trends gathered from trading activity, such as price movement and volume. There are specific terms and statistical models used to describe or characterize the behaviors of indices, share prices, trading volume and so forth. This type of technical analysis can be performed at a market level or for individual stocks, financial instruments and commodities. For more detailed information about technical analysis, the following online discussion provides rich detail.
https://www.investopedia.com/university/technical/

For our purposes here, and in looking at the most recent behavior of the Dow Index, we can focus on two important concepts – support and resistance. Support can be thought of as the lowest value that is "kept" or "maintained" by trading in the Dow Index (or any other financial or market indicator). Resistance is the opposite – the highest level where the market finds resistance. These two concepts form the basis for identifying what's known as trading channels – the area or space between support and resistance. The idea of a trading channel is easy to illustrate with an example (provided by http://StockCharts.com)

The chart for Microsoft's share price (above) covers most of 2016 and has the Channel clearly labeled (left hand side, between the two dashed lines). The dashed line on the top represents resistance and the lower dashed line shows the price for which there is support. The blue arrows demonstrate for you the share prices that are used to identify and measure these two concepts.

In this chart, you will not that the trading channel is nearly horizontal or level across the chart. What this suggests is that for the period covered (the first half of 2016) Microsoft's share price moved sideways. Only after the point labeled "breakout" did the share price move upward, out of the trading channel. When a breakout like this occurs, the theory and assumptions behind technical analysis suggests that a breakout above resistance points to the share price moving upward. If the breakout were to occur below the support line, then the theory would point to future declines in share price.

So how can we use these concepts with the recent behavior of the Dow Index? Going back to the previous charts, let's see what happens when we try to draw lines for resistance and support. For the support level, take a look at the chart below.

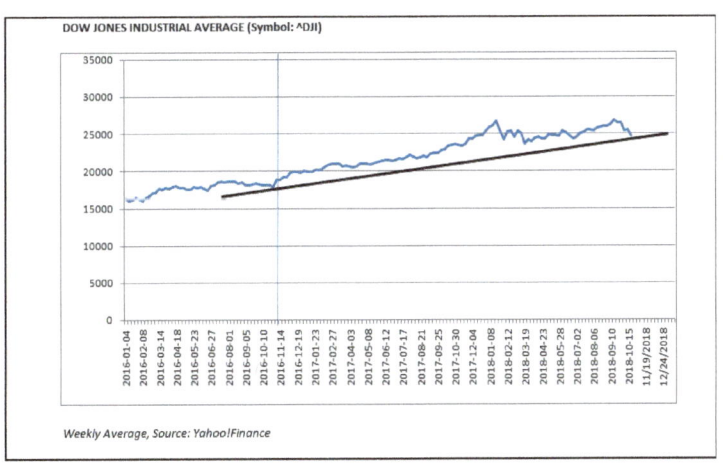

The thicker black line running along the lowest points or bottoms of the Dow Index values over the last couple of years looks like a reasonable support level. This line (straight line regression or rule) shows an indication that there is a good likelihood the Dow will continue to increase the remainder of 2018 and into early 2019.

That opinion, though, hinges on using the low point just before the November 2016 Presidential election as the anchor for drawing (really statistically estimating, but it's easier to understand as "drawing" that line) the support line that connects to the other low points. However, there does appear to be a slightly different support level based only on the Dow Index values since March of 2018 (low value of 23,500 weekly average). Connecting that low point with the other "dips" in the index during the recent sideways movement shows the following.

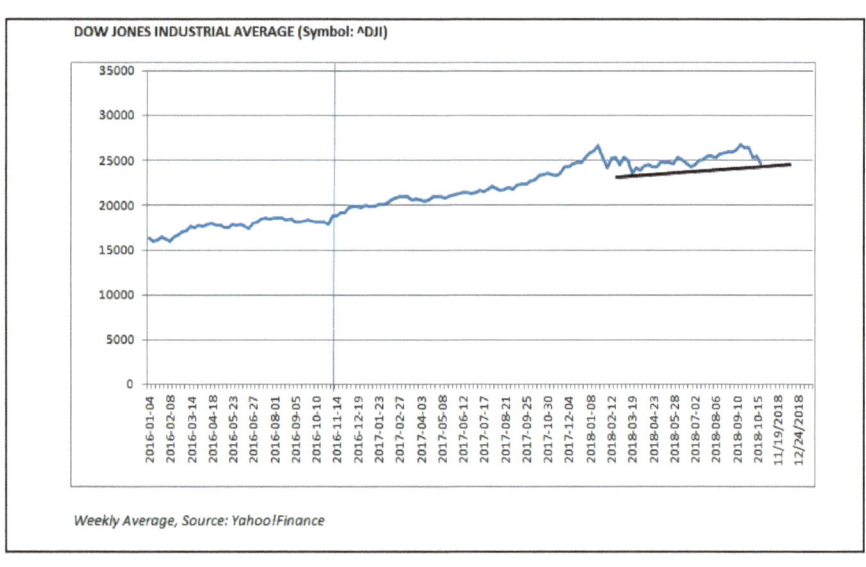

At this shorter resistance line, the anchor or beginning point becomes March 19, 2018 with an index value of 23,533. The results going forward are roughly similar but this shorter trend used to quantify resistance has a slightly lower predicted value at the end of this year.

Assuming that the weekly average Dow Index during the month of November doesn't "break out" to the downside, this resistance level seems to fit the data fairly well. Notice too that the resistance line (estimated statistically) has an upward slope. In our earlier example from Microsoft both the upper and lower lines were flat or non-sloping. Part of what this signals is that the market overall is still growing. In other words the resistance level tends to increase over time along with the overall Dow Index.

Now, what about a support level? Using our same weekly average chart, and starting with the January 2017 period going forward, a support line is relatively easy to estimate.

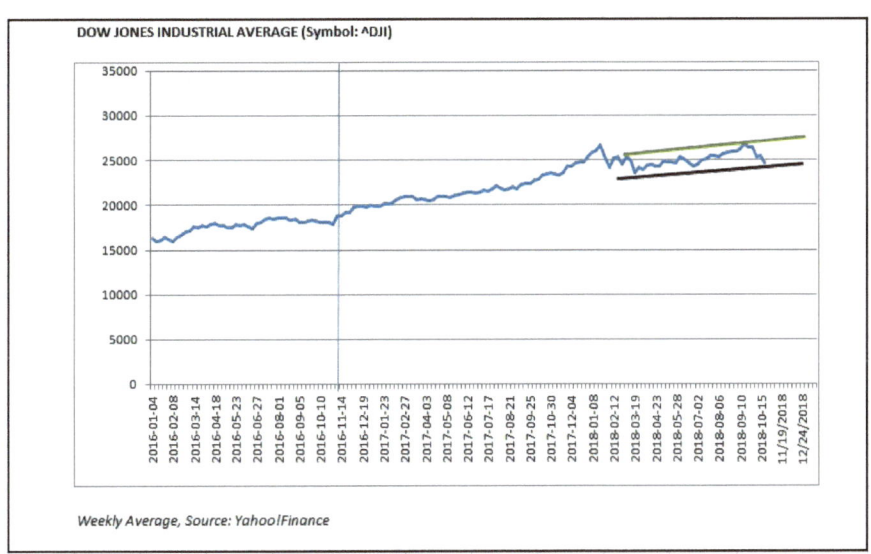

Running roughly parallel to the lower line, our estimated support line (green line in the above chart) connects the peaks over the past 6 or 7 months. Starting at or near the same anchor date as our resistance line, this new support line also trends upward reflecting the growing general market.

The difference between the estimated support line (top, green line) and the estimated resistance line (lower, black line) then becomes our estimated trading channel. If you project the values of these two lines out to the end of 2018 (and actually to the first two weeks of 2019 approximately 12 weeks from the last actual data point we have in the chart), the end result of this trading range is a lower resistance level of 25,136 and an upper support level of 27,603. If the actual value "breaks out" or in other words trades above the support level or trades below the resistance level (typically not just for one week, but for 2-3 weeks in a row), then we'll have a signal of whether this bull market will continue or if we've officially crossed over into bear market territory.

(It's worth noting that the next actual weekly average value that will be added to the chart for week ending November 2, 2018 will be higher than the last one on our charts. The new average will be approximately 25,250, slightly higher. So we know as of this writing that the index has not broken out below resistance. The bull market continues!)

If the Dow Index follows the support trend, and closes the year at or near the support line, the expected or predicted value of the index (27,603) will be almost 12% higher than the lowest value we have from October. According to a recent analysis but MarketWatch (http://marketwatch.com) the stock market increases an average of 14.5% from November to August of the following year, after a mid-term election.

Or, that same article points to other analyses that suggest a shorter term prediction based on past performance would be in the 8-10% range. Based on these analyses, our projected or predicted year-end level based on the top support levels is very reasonable. Our estimated 12% falls just about in the middle of these historical benchmarks. As long as the market or Dow Index continues to trade within the narrow channel set by resistance and support, then today's market will likely replicate or be the same as what's happened in the past.

What about our trend curve? Reapplying the estimated trend curve, we see the complete chart below.

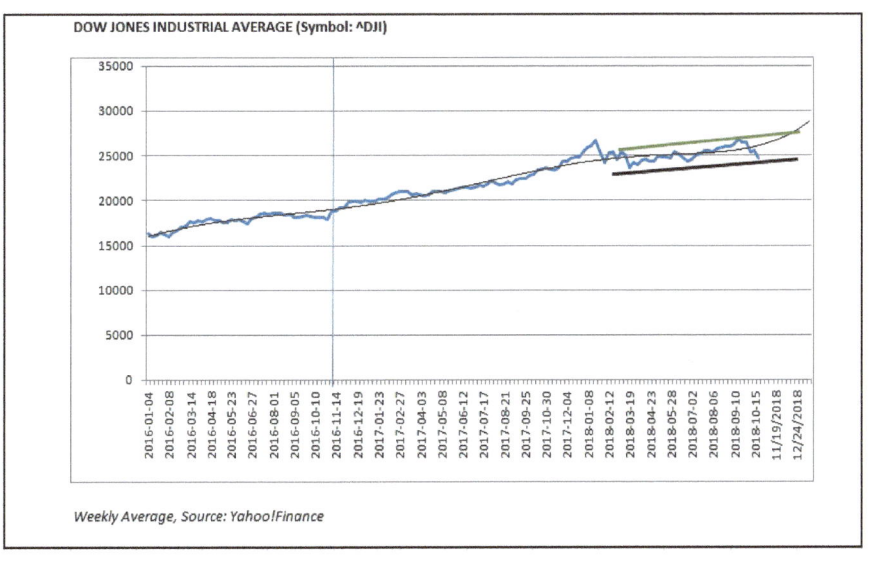

Looking at the black (thinner) trend line, we noted earlier that the curve fits the data well and the model looks robust. Most of the future values on the trend curve (except for the last two weeks) fall within our estimated trading range. These values do tend to be closer to the upside or support line, and if this trend estimate is accurate, the market could well break out above support at the very end of the year or in the first couple of weeks of 2019.

From the trend curve, the last value (12 weeks out) is very close to an index value of 29,000. Difficult to see on the chart above but with a closer look at our statistical models, the predicted trend value winds up about 17% higher than our actual end point. This level of increase would be slightly higher than experienced historically. However, it's still within a "reasonable" level or what some refer to as a reality check. In particular given the positive performance of the US Economy under President Trump, the anticipated results of the mid-term elections, and the recent growth in the stock market, realizing this trend would be a break-out to the upside in the very early weeks of 2019.

That type of break out would signal an even stronger bull market in the coming year. Stock market growth as measured by the Dow Index would continue, at least into 2019. Several fundamental factors might contribute. The President has said he's planning to make tax cuts permanent and to cut taxes further for the American middle class. Business regulations continue to be significantly reduced freeing businesses to invest more, create more jobs and hire more. Wages are starting to increase (+3.1% in October) providing some fuel for consumer spending in the upcoming Holiday season.

So it seems from our analysis – the trend plus support and resistance levels indicate or "predict" continued growth in the Dow Index and overall stock market. If this forecast pans out, and we realize these index levels (29,000) that will represent a bit over 44% higher than at the beginning of 2017 and just over 12% higher than at the beginning of 2018.

Up, down, or sideways? From everything we know today, the November 2018 mid-term elections are set to be in sync with a continued bull market as evidenced by our predicted outcomes for the Dow Index. But there's a little bit of something for everyone in this forecast. Recently, the market has been down. The trend line shows the index continuing to go up, as do our resistance and support lines. And, in the bigger part of the first of 2018, the market actually moved sideways. This is typical for the Dow Jones Index and US Stock Market. We know for certain that the index will go up, go down or move sideways. And within any given period or timeframe, you can usually find evidence of all three.

Summary – Dow Forecast

In sum, we expect the Dow Index to continue increasing from end of October/beginning of November, at least until the early weeks of 2019. November mid-terms are not likely to interfere with that growth. One potential risk comes from any further increases in interest rates by the Fed… something to look out for and keep an eye on. Consistent with past experience and relative to our last October actual value, we expect the Dow Index to increase 12% as our lower estimate or up to 17% as our higher estimate. By early 2019 the Dow Index could be as high as 29,000 but more likely will be closer to and just under 28,000.

9.   Next Steps – What to do with this forecast

Now that we've put together a reasonable case for the expected value of the Dow Index between now and end of the year, what should you do? What next steps are typically taken to maximize your returns based on this forecast?

First, it's important to consider the risks associated with this forecast (or any forecast). What are the risks that our forecast will be wrong? "As soon as you forecast you know you'll be wrong, you just don't know by how much or in which direction," –Edgar Fiedler, The Conference Board

While that quote is funny, there's a ring of truth to it as well. In other words, our forecast could over-predict the level of the Dow Index at the end of this year. Or it could under-predict, where the stock market grows faster than we expect based on our analysis.

To make investment decisions based on our forecast, you should be comfortable with these risks and recognize the level of accuracy built in. We estimate all of our statistical models with a 95% degree of confidence. And the trend model does a good job of explaining variation in the historical data. That's also part of the point too. We estimate these relationships with past data, and the models can be more or less accurate about predicting the future.

We can say definitively though, this same approach and these same types of models were used to accurately predict several key stock market events. What's now known as Black Monday was accurately predicted 6-7 months in advance. We also accurately predicted the significant decline in 2008-9 up to 9 months in advance. And, the recent run up after Trump was elected is part of our accurate forecasting experience as well.

All that means is that you can have a high-degree of confidence in our results. We apply robust tools that have been accurate and proved accurate over time. Nevertheless, things happen. There are outside events that can impact the Dow Index (some of these are what's known as fundamental factors) including events within the United States, as well as events around the world.

You have to assess for yourself how much risk you can live with. The prediction that the Dow Index will close out the year 2018 at or slightly below 29,000 is well-grounded in facts and statistics, and is within reason compared to historical post-mid-term results in the US stock market.

Keeping in mind that the Dow Index reflects the stock market overall, we can also gain additional insights by looking at the 30 individual stocks and the share prices that make up the overall index.

10. Contribution from 30 stocks that make up the Dow Industrial Index

As a reminder, the list of 30 Dow Index stocks and most recent share price for each is in the table below. (Remember each company's trading symbol is in all capitals, first 3 or 4 letters.)

(Ticker Symbol) Company	Share Price	(Ticker Symbol) Company	Share Price
MMM 3M	$ 190.26	JNJ Johnson & Johnson	$ 139.99
AXP American Express	$ 102.73	JPM JPMorgan Chase	$ 109.02
AAPL Apple	$ 218.86	MCD McDonald's	$ 176.90
BA Boeing	$ 354.86	MRK Merck	$ 73.61
CAT Caterpillar	$ 121.32	MSFT Microsoft	$ 106.81
CVX Chevron	$ 111.65	NKE Nike	$ 75.04
CSCO Cisco	$ 45.75	PFE Pfizer	$ 43.06
KO Coca-Cola	$ 47.88	PG Procter & Gamble	$ 88.68
DIS Disney	$ 114.83	TRV Travelers Companies Inc	$ 125.13
DWDP DowDuPont Inc	$ 53.92	UTX United Technologies	$ 124.21
XOM Exxon Mobil	$ 79.68	UNH UnitedHealth	$ 261.35
GS Goldman Sachs	$ 225.37	VZ Verizon	$ 57.09
HD Home Depot	$ 175.88	V Visa	$ 137.85
IBM IBM	$ 115.43	WMT Wal-Mart	$ 100.28
INTC Intel	$ 46.88	WBA Walgreen	$ 79.77

For each of these stocks, there are key periods of time we can analyze to see if they behave "like" the overall index or not. The stocks that have share price changes (up, down or sideways) closest to the overall index will be the best representatives and may be likely to have similar trends as well as resistance and support.

Recalling that the support line for the Dow Index overall started with the anchor period of March 12th and covered the weeks up to and including September 17th, we can show how each share price as well as the overall index performed. For example, the Dow Index increased just over 7% during that period. Now let's look at the changes for each stock.

Percent Change in Share Price
March 12, 2018 to September 17, 2018
By individual stock share price

Symbol	Company	Percent Change Mar 12 - Sept 17
AAPL	Apple	23.2
AXP	American Express	16.8
BA	Boeing	13.8
CAT	Caterpillar	1.1
CSCO	Cisco	9.6
CVX	Chevron	6.9
DIS	Disney	8.2
DWDP	DowDuPont Inc	3.7
GS	Goldman Sachs	-11.5
HD	Home Depot	20.0
IBM	IBM	-3.5
INTC	Intel	-7.7
JNJ	Johnson & Johnson	8.4
JPM	JPMorgan Chase	3.2
KO	Coca-Cola	10.0
MCD	McDonald's	3.1
MMM	3M	-7.6
MRK	Merck	30.7
MSFT	Microsoft	21.8
NKE	Nike	30.5
PFE	Pfizer	22.0
PG	Procter & Gamble	10.7
TRV	Travelers Companies Inc	-3.7
UNH	UnitedHealth	17.8
UTX	United Technologies	11.9
V	Visa	20.9
VZ	Verizon	14.8
WBA	Walgreen	9.4
WMT	Wal-Mart	8.9
XOM	Exxon Mobil	15.7
^DJI	Dow Jones Industrial Index	7.2

Organized alphabetically rather than by share price or percent change, the table above shows there are a handful of stocks out of the group of 30 that had similar increases during this period – increases in share price that were similar to the increase in the overall Dow Index.

For example, Chevron share price increased 6.9 percent and Johnson & Johnson share price rose 8.4 percent. These changes compare to the overall index increase of 7.2 percent. One of the next things to do then will be to look at the patterns over time in the share prices of these stocks to check and see if we can estimate similar resistance and support lines.

The table above also shows, however, that quite a few stocks reported gains in share prices significantly higher than the overall index. Many of these increased 15% or more, over twice the value for the index total. Also, though, there were also stocks whose share prices changed a lot less than the overall and there were even several that reported declining share prices during this period.

This graph represents the data visually.

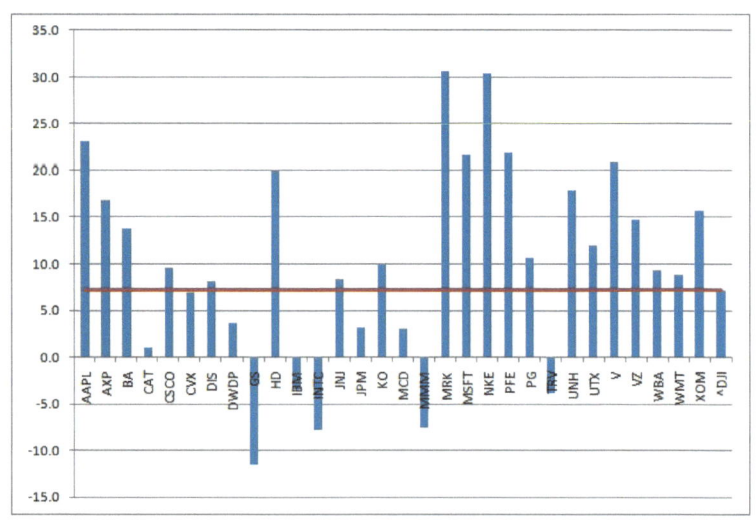

And turns out about half of the 30 stocks reported percent changes for this period over the index total of 7.2 (red straight line) and about half reported percent changes that were less than overall. This is one of the key characteristics of averages or weighted averages like the one known as the Dow Industrial Index. The market overall and changes in its level typically represents some type of mid-point of the distribution of share prices and changes in share prices at the individual company level.

One other way to examine these 30 stocks would be to go through the same level of trend and technical analysis for each one. For purposes of demonstration, we'll take a look at the two stocks closest to the change in the overall index, Chevron and Johnson & Johnson.

The chart below shows the behavior of the Johnson & Johnson share price over the same time period we've been using to evaluate the overall Dow Index.

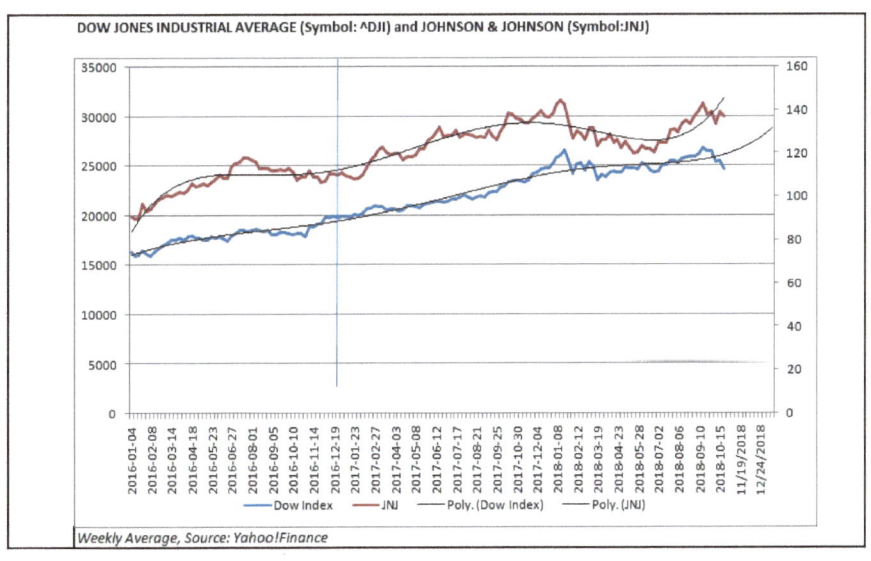

Notice that the Johnson & Johnson share price is plotted on the right-hand scale. This adjustment or added dimension allows us to see the share price plotted over time. If we tried to plot it on the same scale as the Dow Index, all the graph points would be unreadable and very close to the zero axis.

You can see from the chart above that the trend patterns of the Johnson & Johnson share price closely follow trends in the overall Dow Index, until the peak weekly average value at the beginning of 2018. After that, the Johnson & Johnson share price fell more than the Dow, and then increased more than the Dow up to the next peak during the week of September 17th. After September, the Johnson & Johnson share price has not fallen as much as the overall Dow.

Naturally since the Johnson & Johnson share price is one of the 30 components of the overall Dow Industrial Average, it's expected that the two will behave similarly. The Dow though is influenced by 29 other stocks and their per unit share price. Compared to the Dow Index overall, Johnson & Johnson's share price has a similar trend, but it increases more rapidly during the latest weeks than the Dow trend.

And we can show resistance and support level for the Johnson & Johnson share price. The chart below shows these new estimates for the single company as well as placing the earlier estimates for the Dow in total back on the chart.

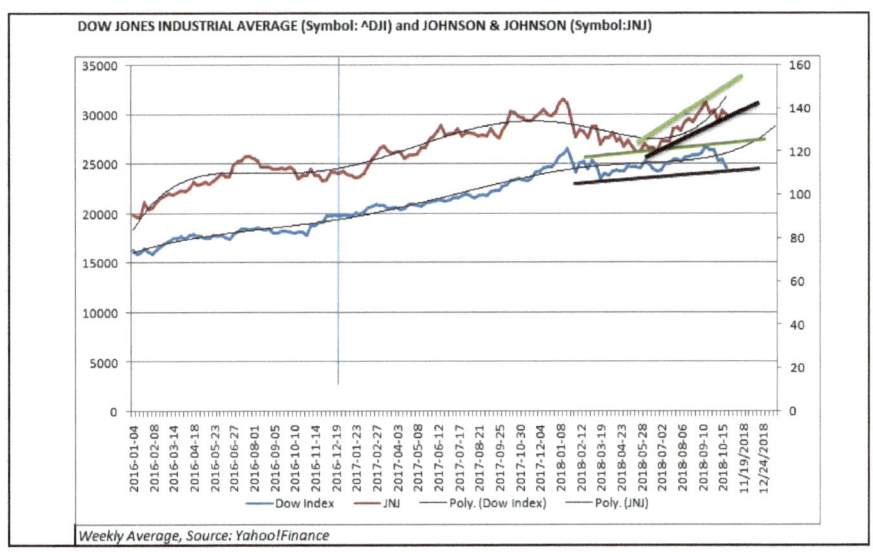

You'll note that there are distinct differences for Johnson & Johnson support, resistance and the estimated trading channel vs. the Dow Index overall.

First, the time period used to estimate the resistance and support lines is shorter for the individual company share price than for the Dow Index overall. This makes sense in part due to the fact that the Index represents the behavior of all 30 stocks and is therefore influenced by many different technical and trend behaviors.

Second, there does not appear to be a time period when the share price of the Johnson & Johnson stock moved sideways. There was a clear move down after the peak in early 2018, then a falling up period.

Finally, the trading channel estimated appears to widen over time, rather than remain constant. The implication of this is that the support level is increasing while the resistance level is decreasing, at the same time. Looking at that widening trade channel, it appears the share price will end the year 2018 just under $160 (USD) per share.

Chevron's share price compared to the Dow Index average is shown in the chart below.

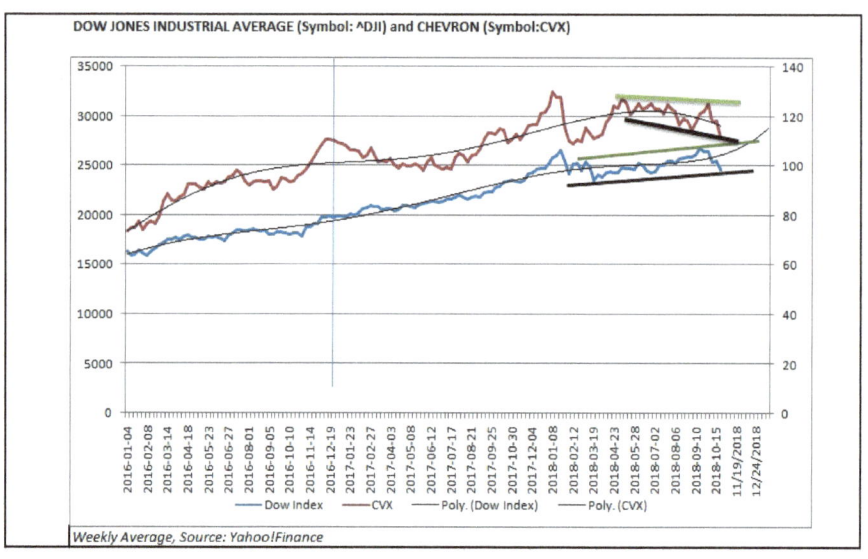

This chart includes the actual share price for the same period of time we've been using, plotted on the right-hand scale. And, the trend plus resistance and support lines have been estimated and added to the chart.

For Chevron, the share value followed overall market behavior and trends for most of 2016 and 2017, with a peak value at about the same time as the Dow Index overall – the beginning of 2018. After that, though, the individual share price behaves differently than either the Dow Index in total or our other individual company share price, Johnson & Johnson.

Specifically, the share price of Chevron (CVX) starts a downward trend after mid-May 2018. Note here also that the trading channel defined by the resistance and support lines widens over time due to the support line declining week to week. The resistance line (green) also declines but much more gradually than the lower support line (black).

Based on the downward trend and the defined trading channel, it looks like the share price of Chevron is headed toward ending the year a little over $110 (USD) per share. The declining share price trend and the predicted decline to a year-end value of $110 is in stark contrast to both Johnson & Johnson and the Dow Index in total – both of which are increasing.

At this point in our analysis it's worth saying that each of the 30 companies and their share prices that make up the Dow Index has its own behavior, trends, as well as estimates of resistance and support. To get a true understanding of which of the 30 companies appears to be driving more of the predicted increase in the Dow by year's end, we would need to analyze and evaluate each individual stock.

That detailed level of analysis could then be used to build a case for supporting the overall analysis of the Dow Index. In other words, if (for example) 25 of the 30 stocks show similar trends and increasing trade channels, then we could say that the overall health of the stock market is pretty good. The expected increases between now and the end of 2018 would appear to be robust and occurring throughout the different sectors of the economy represented by the Dow.

If we find that there are more disparate results and more variance among the individual stocks and how they perform, then it would likely be accurate to say the predicted outcomes for the Dow Index are more a function of a few strong performing stocks rather than the market overall.

Going into 2019, this would be an important perspective to have. However, diving into an analysis of each of the 30 stocks that make up the Dow Index is beyond the scope of this current book. We will do the additional analysis and publish it along with these overall market findings on Amazon as well. For now, though, let's return to the subject of how we expect the stock market to perform after the November 2018 mid-term elections.

Our work here has showed that we expect the Dow Index to continue increasing from end of October/beginning of November, through the end of 2018 and into the early weeks of 2019. November mid-terms are not likely to interfere with that growth and in fact can be seen as a source of support for that growth. Historically, after mid-term elections the stock market as represented by the Dow Index has increased between 11% and 15%. Our models and analysis show an expected increase in the Dow Index value to just below 28,000, an increase of almost 14% from its level at the end of October.

So if the question is, "Will the stock market move up, down, or sideways after the November 2018 mid-terms?", our definitive answer is "UP".

Author's Note:

Please keep in mind that the behaviors of individual company share prices – the 30 companies that make of the Dow – will vary from the market overall.

This manuscript focuses on technical and trend analysis of the Dow Index, relative to the mid-November elections. As such, we've ignored another fruitful type of analysis that is typically used called fundamental analysis. Fundamental analysis looks at economic and macro factors that are expected to have an impact on the markets (or individual share prices) and then create a forecast from what is known about those impacts.

This is a more detailed and sometimes complicated type of analysis, but it can be as accurate or more accurate than our technical analysis. And, if you combine technical and fundamental analyses, that's usually thought to be the best of all possible outcomes. We will address fundamental analysis and how it affects our Dow forecasts in a future manuscript.

A brief bio for Mr. Allman:

Dale Allman has substantial experience in economics, forecasting and marketing. He is a former Economist with the Federal Reserve Bank in Kansas City and has over 15 years experience in leadership roles at Hallmark Cards, Intuit and other Fortune 500 US companies.

His brand experience includes the following clients: Duracell, Quaker Oats, The Minute Maid Company, Visa, Zurich International, Baylor Healthcare, American Airlines, The Dallas Morning News and others.

He is very well-versed in SEM, simultaneous equations, factor analysis, forecasting and predictive modeling, neural networks, logistic regression, and CHAID to name a few techniques. Dale has been recognized and published in several trade and professional venues throughout his career. His work in marketing mix models was recognized at the ARTS Forum of the American Marketing Association. His analyses and publications have been featured in The New York Times, Financial Analysts Journal, and The Economic Review of the Federal Reserve Bank of Kansas City.

www.ingramcontent.com/pod-product-compliance
Lightning Source LLC
Chambersburg PA
CBHW040337220526
45473CB00009B/2713